EARTH SCIENCE DETECTIVES

Investigating
Fault Lines

Miriam Coleman

New York

Published in 2016 by The Rosen Publishing Group, Inc.
29 East 21st Street, New York, NY 10010

First Edition

Editor: Sarah Machajewski
Book Design: Katelyn Heinle

Photo Credits: Cover Kevin Schafer/Minden Pictures/Getty Images; pp. 4, 22 Lee Prince/Shutterstock.com; p. 5 James Balog/The Image Bank/Getty Images; p. 7 Lukiyanova Natalia/frenta/Shutterstock.com; p. 8 Aleksandar Mijatovic/Shutterstock.com; p. 9 Dorling Kindersley/Getty Images; p. 10 © iStockphoto.com/wanlorn; p. 11 NigelSpiers/Shutterstock.com; p. 12 Naeblys/Shutterstock.com; p. 13 De Agostini/Publiaer Foto/De Agostini Picture Library/Getty Images; p. 14 Dr. Morley Read/Shutterstock.com; p. 15 daulon/Shutterstock.com; p. 17 S.J. Krasemann/Photolibrary/Getty Images; p. 18 http://commons.wikimedia.org/wiki/File:FaultGouge.JPG; p. 19 http://commons.wikimedia.org/wiki/File:Pseudotachylite_Breccia_of_Vredefort_in_South_Africa.jpg; p. 21 karamysh/Shutterstock.com.

Coleman, Miriam, author.
 Investigating fault lines / Miriam Coleman.
     pages cm. — (Earth science detectives)
 Includes bibliographical references and index.
 ISBN 978-1-4777-5939-4 (pbk.)
 ISBN 978-1-4777-5940-0 (6 pack)
 ISBN 978-1-4777-5938-7 (library binding)
 1. Faults (Geology)—Juvenile literature. 2. Earthquakes—Juvenile literature. 3. Plate tectonics—Juvenile literature. I. Title. II. Series:
Coleman, Miriam.
 QE606.C58 2015
 551.8′72—dc23
                          2014031924

Manufactured in the United States of America

CPSIA Compliance Information: Batch #WS15PK: For Further Information contact Rosen Publishing, New York, New York at 1-800-237-9932

CONTENTS

CLUES IN THE GROUND

The ground may appear to be solid, but Earth's surface is constantly moving and changing shape. We can't always feel it, but scientists know how to look for clues that show where, when, and how Earth's surface moves.

Geologists are scientists who study Earth and the forces that change it. They're like detectives, looking for clues in the **landscape** to solve mysteries about our planet. Sometimes they find clues on the ground that show what's happening far below Earth's surface. They're called fault lines. What can they tell us about Earth?

The two blocks of rock on either side of this fault line were once joined together. What caused this giant crack to form?

This crack in the ground is called a fault line. Read on to find out how and why such lines form.

INSIDE EARTH

Imagine the first people who came across fault lines. They may not have known the lines were signs of activity happening below Earth's surface. Over time, geologists figured out the cracks could help them understand what the inside of our planet is like.

Scientists often separate Earth into **layers**. The core is in the center. The middle layer is the mantle. Part of the mantle is made of soft rock, and part of the mantle is solid. Earth's outermost layer is the crust. Together, the solid upper mantle and the crust form the lithosphere. This is where movement inside Earth begins.

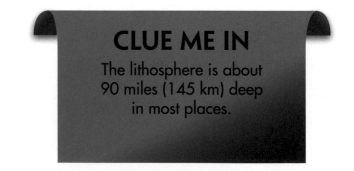

CLUE ME IN

The lithosphere is about 90 miles (145 km) deep in most places.

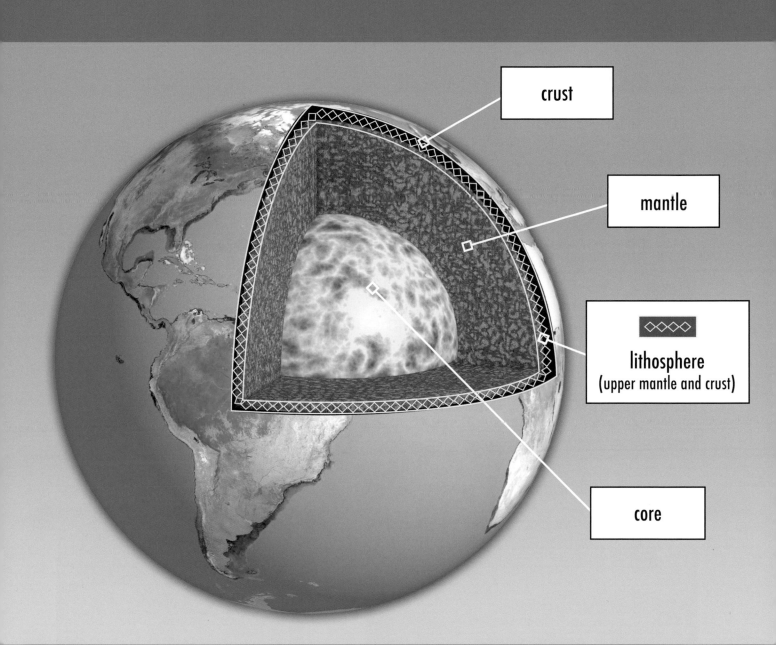

crust

mantle

lithosphere
(upper mantle and crust)

core

The lithosphere floats on top of the mantle's soft layer. This causes the lithosphere to move very slowly.

A PUZZLE OF PLATES

Geologists believe the lithosphere is made of large pieces called tectonic (tehk-TAH-nihk) plates. The plates fit together like a puzzle. The giant pieces move slowly as they float on the mantle's soft rock layer.

The movement of the plates creates **stress**, which travels through Earth's crust and sometimes cracks it. A crack or break in the crust is called a fault. A fault line is a crack that reaches Earth's surface. Scientists see fault lines as **evidence** that the plates below them are moving because fault lines are often found in areas where two plates meet.

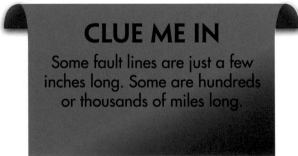

CLUE ME IN
Some fault lines are just a few inches long. Some are hundreds or thousands of miles long.

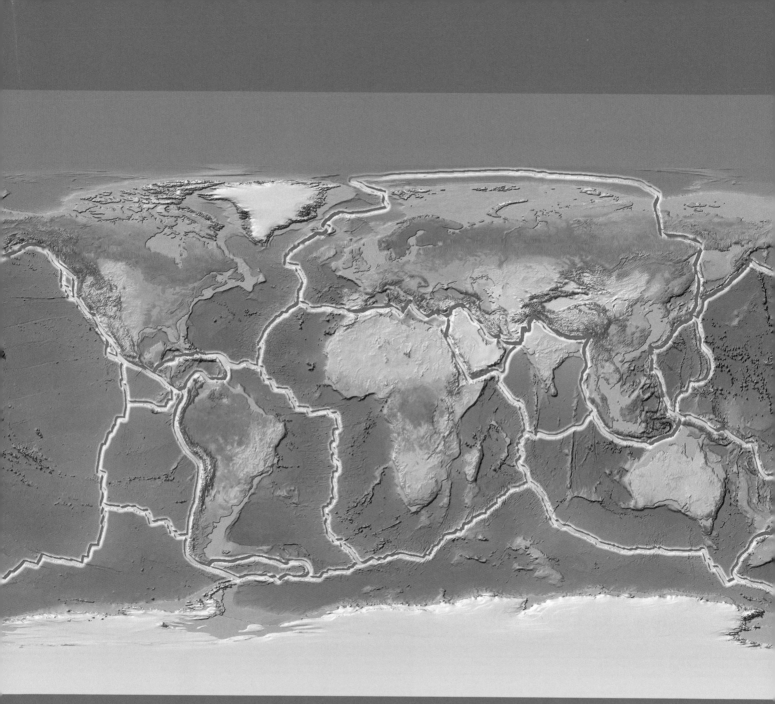

The place where two tectonic plates meet is called a boundary.

The movement of Earth's plates can lead to some amazing **geological** events, including earthquakes. Earthquakes occur when two plates try to slide past each other but can't. Stress builds up until the rocks can no longer hold it. The giant masses of rock snap free from each other. The sudden release of **energy** travels through the earth in the form of **vibrations** that cause the ground to shake.

Scientists call these vibrations seismic (SYZ-mihk) waves. Scientists measure seismic waves on a machine called a seismograph. Their findings tell them where the earthquake started and how big it was.

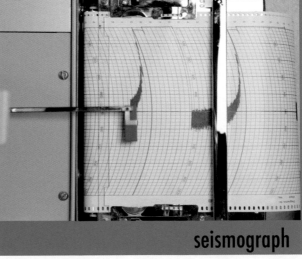

seismograph

CLUE ME IN

Earthquakes occur along faults. Sometimes an earthquake happening is the first time people learn there's a fault in an area.

Scientists use the Richter scale to measure an earthquake's energy. The Richter scale goes from 1.0 to 10. Earthquakes that reach 10 are rare, but very destructive.

STRIKE-SLIP FAULTS

Scientists name a fault by how the sections of Earth on either side of it move against each other. A strike-slip fault occurs when two blocks of rock move past each other **horizontally**. Strike-slip faults on the boundary between two plates are called transform faults.

One of the most famous transform faults is the San Andreas Fault in California. It marks the boundary between the Northern Pacific Plate and the North American Plate. Scientists study this fault to learn how it's changed California's landscape. Studying the earthquakes that happen there helps scientists predict how the land will change in the future.

strike-slip fault

CLUE ME IN

The San Andreas Fault is about 28 million years old. It's over 800 miles (1,287 km) long!

Many earthquakes happen along the San Andreas Fault. In 1906, a powerful earthquake hit San Francisco. Scientists didn't fully understand faults or fault lines at that time, so they were surprised at how the ground moved horizontally and how long the crack was.

DIP-SLIP FAULTS

Another type of fault is called a dip-slip fault. It occurs when forces pull apart or squeeze together Earth's crust. This causes the blocks of rock to shift up or down.

The block above the sloping fault line before the blocks shift is called the hanging wall. The block below the sloping fault line is called the footwall. When the crust is pulled apart, the hanging wall moves down. This is a normal fault. When the crust is squeezed together, the hanging wall is pushed up over the footwall. This is a reverse fault.

The shifting sides of a dip-slip fault can show different kinds of rocks or rocks from different geological periods. Scientists study the rocks to learn what that part of Earth is made of and how old it is.

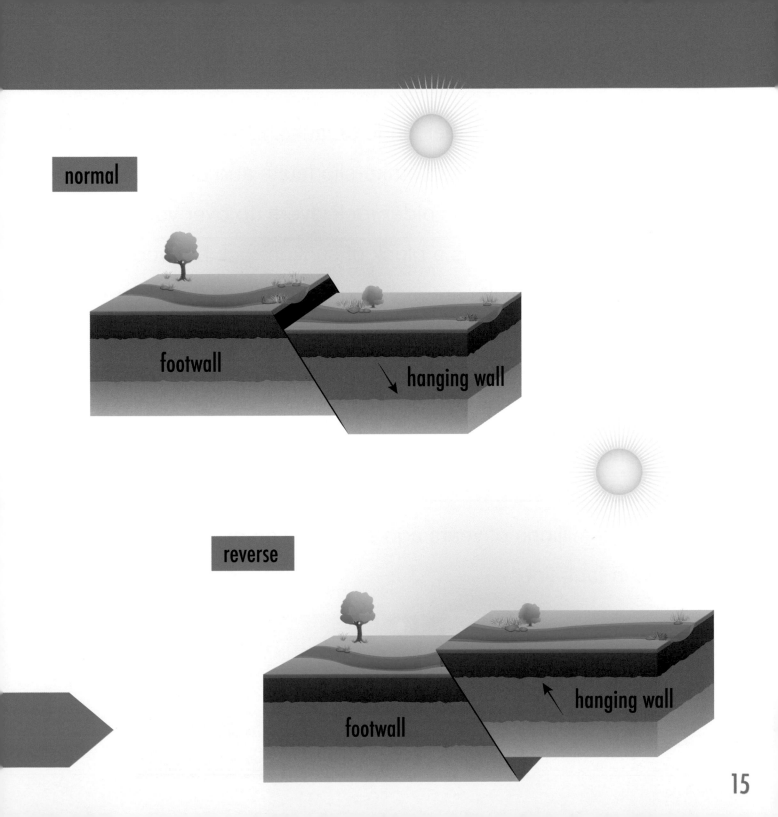

normal

footwall

hanging wall

reverse

footwall

hanging wall

There are many other kinds of faults. Oblique-slip faults combine features of strike-slip faults and dip-slip faults. Thrust faults push older rock layers up over younger rock layers. A graben is a block of sunken rock between two faults. Ring faults are many normal faults in the shape of a circle. They form where rocks have caved in after a **volcano** explodes.

These faults tell us a lot about changes that have happened on Earth, even if we weren't around to see them. Geologists have learned a lot about events that occurred millions of years ago simply by studying the clues in fault lines.

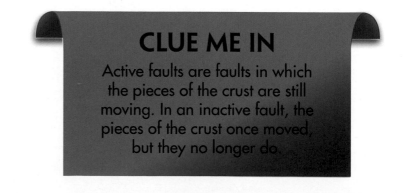

CLUE ME IN

Active faults are faults in which the pieces of the crust are still moving. In an inactive fault, the pieces of the crust once moved, but they no longer do.

Thrust faults in the northern Rocky Mountains have uncovered layers of rock that have been "folded" by Earth's forces. The Folded Mountain, shown here, is located in British Columbia, Canada.

FAULT ROCK

As the lithosphere moves, the force crushes and grinds the rocky crust to create cataclastic rock. One type of cataclastic rock is fault breccia (BREH-chee-uh), which is made of large pieces of rock. Fault gouge is another kind. It's made of rock that's been ground into a fine powder.

Pseudotachylite (soo-doh-TAA-kih-lyt) can look like black glass and is often found as lines in a fault wall. It's usually formed when powerful fault movements cause rocks in the fault wall to melt. When geologists find pseudotachylite, it's a clue that an earthquake may have happened in that spot.

fault gouge

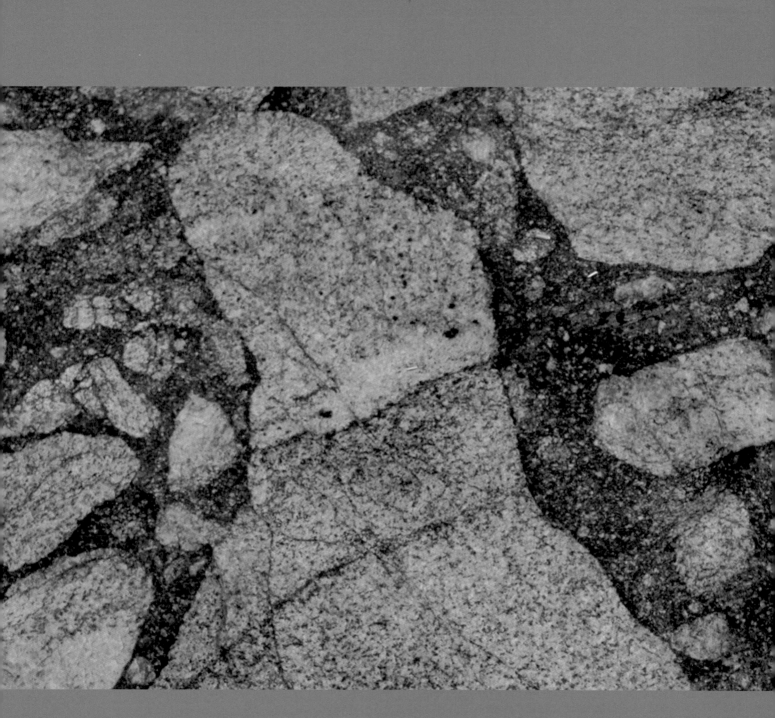

Pseudotachylite is black and can appear glassy.

HOW FAULTS CHANGE THE LAND

Faults play a major role in how our world looks. Normal faults create flat areas of land, while reverse faults squeeze Earth's surface to create beautiful mountain ranges. The Andes Mountains in South America were formed when the South American Plate crashed into a smaller plate in the Pacific Ocean, which lifted up the land.

When earthquakes occur in places where lots of people live, it can be very bad. The shaking can knock down buildings and destroy roads as well as gas and water lines. The worst earthquakes in history have killed hundreds of thousands of people.

Fault lines have taught us a lot about Earth, from things we can see, such as mountains, to things we can't see, such as the inside of the planet.

CLUE ME IN

Fault lines are often covered by lots of soil, sand, or gravel. Scientists can tell they're there, though, if rocks that normally wouldn't be together are in the same area. Scientists guess that fault activity brought them together.

READING FAULT LINE CLUES

Fault lines are important because they can tell us a lot about the powerful forces at work far below the surface of our planet. By studying faults and fault lines, geologists can also gain clues about how Earth will change in the future.

If a fault line tells us that more earthquakes are likely to come to an area, we can build our cities to be strong when the ground shakes. We can also imagine what our world will be like many years in the future. What else can fault lines tell us?

GLOSSARY

energy: The power to do work.

evidence: Facts, signs, or information that proves something to be true.

geological: Having to do with the science that deals with Earth, its history, and the processes that act on it.

horizontal: Side to side.

landscape: The visible features of an area of land.

layer: One thickness lying over or under another.

stress: The force put on an object.

vibration: Fast movement up and down or back and forth.

volcano: An opening in Earth's surface through which hot, liquid rock sometimes flows.

INDEX

WEBSITES

Due to the changing nature of Internet links, PowerKids Press has developed an online list of websites related to the subject of this book. This site is updated regularly. Please use this link to access the list: www.powerkidslinks.com/det/faul